CRANES

HEAVY EQUIPMENT

David and Patricia Armentrout

The Rourke Book Co., Inc.
Vero Beach, Florida 32964

PHOTO CREDITS
© Armentrout: pages 4, 10, 13, 18, 21; © East Coast Studios:
Cover, Title page, pages 7, 8, 12, 15; © NASA page 17

ACKNOWLEDGEMENTS
The authors would like to thank Airborne Express for their help in
the preparation of this book

Library of Congress Cataloging-in-Publication Data

Armentrout, Patricia, 1960-
    Cranes / by Patricia Armentrout and David Armentrout.
        p. cm. — (Heavy Equipment)
    Includes index.
    ISBN 1-55916-133-7
    1. Cranes, derricks etc.—Juvenile literature.   [1. Cranes. 2.
derricks etc.]
I. Armentrout, David, 1962- .   II. Title.   III. Series: Armentrout,
Patricia, 1960-   Heavy Equipment.
TJ1363.A75 1995
621.8' 7—dc20   95–3979
                                                          CIP
                                                           AC

Printed in the USA

TABLE OF CONTENTS

What Are Cranes?   5
Block and Tackle   6
Mobile Cranes   9
Crane Attachments   11
Jib Cranes   14
Crane Operators   16
Straddle Cranes   19
Truck Cranes   20
Derricks   22
Glossary   23
Index   24

WHAT ARE CRANES?

Cranes are load lifters. They are used to move heavy objects.

Cranes are seen every day at construction sites. They lift and move building materials. Waterfront docks have huge cranes that load and unload **cargo** (KAR go) ships. You may see a crane with a wrecking ball, sometimes called a "scull cracker," destroying an old building.

Cranes vary in size and do many different jobs. Some are built for just one job.

A magnet attachment hangs from the load line of this stationary crane

BLOCK AND TACKLE

Block and tackle is another way of saying **pulleys** (PUL eez) and cables. A pulley is a grooved wheel. The cable is placed in the groove and around the wheel.

When you pull down on the cable, you lift up what is attached to the other end. The pulley and cable takes on some of the weight of the object lifted.

The pulley and cable, or block and tackle, is used to do the heavy load lifting on cranes.

Some construction sites are so large that several cranes are in use at the same time

MOBILE CRANES

Some cranes move across the ground on crawler treads the way bulldozers and army tanks do. These cranes are mobile cranes.

A mobile crane has a long arm called a **boom** (boom) that extends into the air. The boom helps to support the pulleys and cables as the crane lifts its heavy load.

Mobile cranes move throughout the work site dangling a large hook at the end of the cable, or load line. The hook is used to lift loads of lumber, metal beams, and sections of wall or roof.

Large mobile cranes move around the work site lifting various building materials

CRANE ATTACHMENTS

An attachment can turn a crane into a giant digger. A bucket attachment can dig soil from under water and move it to the shore line. A digger such as the backhoe cannot extend over the water like the moveable boom on a crane.

Auto junk yards and metal recycling stations can use cranes with a giant magnet attachment. The magnet at the end of the load line can pick up a junk car or truck and drop it into a crushing bin.

Junk yard cranes use grapple attachments that can grasp large clumps of scrap metal

This crane lifts construction materials and supplies to workers on top of the building

Block and tackle hang from an overhead crane

JIB CRANES

All cranes have moveable parts. A jib crane has a rotating boom called a jib. The jib can move in a circle to set its load in an exact spot.

A jib crane is used in some machine shops. These smaller cranes use a platform or bucket at the end of the load line. Heavy equipment or tools can be moved to different locations in the shop.

Aircraft mechanics use a jib crane to lift heavy loads like this jet engine

CRANE OPERATORS

Crane operators move levers with their hands and pedals with their feet. The pedals and levers are used to move all the crane's lifting equipment.

The operator rotates the crane into position, lowers the load line, raises the boom, and controls all movements of the attachments.

Crane operators must know exactly how much weight their machine can lift safely.

An overhead crane is used to remove a space shuttle from the top of a NASA jet

STRADDLE CRANES

Straddle cranes **straddle** (STRAD el) the load to be lifted. Some have large wheels that move the crane over the cargo.

The stacker crane is also a straddle crane. It is used at cargo ship docks to stack large containers. Some straddle cranes can lift as much as 500,000 pounds!

Railroad yards use a type of straddle crane called a gantry. The gantry crane rides on rails instead of wheels. It is used to lift and move railroad cars.

Rail yards use gantry cranes to lift heavy tractor trailers on and off train cars

TRUCK CRANES

Truck cranes are very useful because they can travel to work sites whenever needed. Since truck cranes share roadways with smaller vehicles, they have a boom that can be made shorter or longer as needed. Some truck cranes have booms that extend from 30 feet to 200 feet by inserting extensions.

Truck cranes need added support for heavy load lifting. They are equipped with metal legs called **outriggers** (OUT RIG erz). Outriggers reach from the sides of the truck and extend down to the ground to provide a wider base.

Truck cranes are commonly used by utility companies to lift engineers up to the electric wires

DERRICKS

Some cranes are built to stay in one place. These cranes are called derricks.

Guy derricks have cable wires holding the center support beam, or **mast** (mast), in place. Guy derricks have moveable booms and load lines like mobile cranes.

Stiff-legged derricks are seen at construction sites. They have metal legs that are fastened to the ground. The legs, called **girders** (GER derz), support the boom and attachments that the load line carries.

Glossary

boom (boom) — an arm that helps to support the load a crane or derrick is lifting

cargo (KAR go) — goods carried in a vehicle

girders (GER derz) — main support beams on derricks

mast (mast) — a pole that supports beams and ropes or cables

outriggers (OUT RIG erz) — metal legs attached to truck cranes that act as extra support when the crane is in use

pulleys (PUL eez) — grooved wheels that hold a rope or cable

straddle (STRAD el) — to stand over or above with open legs or support beams

INDEX

block and tackle   6
boom   9, 11, 14, 16, 20, 22
bucket   11, 14
cable   6, 9, 22
cargo   5, 19
crane operator   16
derricks   22
gantry crane   19
girders   22
hook   9
jib crane   14

load line   9, 11, 14, 16, 22
magnet   11
mast   22
mobile cranes   9, 22
outriggers   20
platform   14
pulley   6, 9
stacker crane   19
straddle   19
treads   9
truck cranes   20
wrecking ball   5